My Pretty COLORING BOOK

Thank you for choosing

We create our books with great love and care yet mistakes beyond our control can happen in printing, binding and shipping. If you have any questions, comments, concerns, or problems with this book please contact us at: bluejewelbooks@gmail.com.

Published by Blue Jewel Books

FLOWERS

Made in the USA
Las Vegas, NV
13 December 2024

13873566R00063